Pump it up Magazine

TABLE OF CONTENTS

⚡ **EDITORIAL**
Page 5

⚡ **NEW YEAR NEW YOU!**
- DIY POST WORKOUT
- BOOS TO MAKE YOU FEEL GOOD
- VACATIONS SPOT
- 8 MANTRAS TO MAKE YOU FEEL GOOD

⚡ **WELLNESS**
BREAK FREE FROM NARCISSISTIC ABUSE

⚡ **CINEMA**
Healing Through Films

6 ⚡ **LINC HAND**
BALANCING ACTING & FITNESS SUCCESS

13 ⚡ **FITNESS**
PUMP UP YOUR WORKOUT WITH OUR PLAYLIST AND FITNESS PLAN

24 ⚡ **TOP TIPS**
FOR TAKING CARE OF YOUR MENTAL HEALTH

26 ⚡ **HUMANITARIAN AWARENESS**
- HONORING DR. MARTIN LUTHER KING JR. SUPPORTING BLACK COMMUNITIES AND HOW YOU CAN HELP

Pump it up
MAGAZINE

PUMP IT UP MAGAZINE
LINKS

WEBSITE
www.pumpitupmagazine.com

FACEBOOK
www.facebook.com/pumpitupmagazine

TWITTER
www.twitter.com/pumpitupmag

SOUNDCLOUD
www.soundcloud.com/pumpitupmagazine

INSTAGRAM
pumpitupmagazine

PINTEREST
www.pinterest.com/pumpitupmagazine

PUMP IT UP MAGAZINE
30721 Russell Ranch Road
Suite 140
Westlake Village,
California 91362
United States

 (818)514 – 0038(Ext:102)
 info@pumpitupmagazine.com

Letter from the Editor

Hey there, Fabulous Readers,

I'm beyond thrilled to welcome you to the newest edition of our magazine – a concoction of passion, dedication, and a dash of unyielding pursuit for awesomeness!

In this issue, we've cooked up a delightful blend of articles aimed at nurturing personal growth and wellness. From the wisdom of Linc Hand on juggling acting (with Harrison Ford "42" movie and lately NCISHawaii) and fitness triumphs to playlists that'll kick your workout into high gear, we're here to pump up your journey to a healthier, happier you.

And with the dawn of a new year, we're all about transformation in our "New Year, New You!" segment, complete with tips and heartfelt advice on breaking free from anything toxic.

Wellness is our jam, so we've dedicated sections to guide you through self-care rituals, soul-soothing reads, dreamy vacations, and the magic of movies.

In this edition, we honor Dr. Martin Luther King Jr.'s legacy by shedding light on ways to support and uplift Black communities.

We hope these pages spark inspiration, prompt a bit of self-reflection, and provide a haven in the midst of life's whirlwind.

Your journey to a better self starts right here, within these pages.

Thanks a million for letting us be part of your journey.
Together, let's dive into growth, celebrate diversity, and champion resilience.

Happy New Year 🧡

Your Friendly Editor-in-Chief,

Anissa Sutton

CONTRIBUTORS

FOUNDER & EDITOR IN CHIEF
Anissa Sutton

EDITOR
Michael B. Sutton

MARKETING
Grace Rose

PARTNERS

Editions L.A.
www.editions-la.com

The Sound Of L.A.
www.thesoundofla.com

Info Music
www.infomusic.fr

YMC
yourmusicconsultant.com

Cover Magazine Photo credit:
Travon Hodges

LINC HAND: NAVIGATING HOLLYWOOD'S LIMELIGHT WITH ATHLETICISM, ACTING, AND ADVENTURE

Born and bred in the enchanting ambiance of Birmingham, Alabama, Linc Hand embarked on his journey into the limelight at the tender age of six. His charismatic presence has graced commercials, television screens, and feature films, creating ripples of admiration within the entertainment realm.

Upon venturing to Los Angeles, Linc immersed himself deeper into his passion for acting, guided by the legendary coach Howard Fine. The intersection of innate talent and cultivated skill marked th inception of a remarkable career.

A genuine enthusiast of athleticism, Linc's early love for sports, instilled by his father, propelled him to excel in football, basketball, and martial arts. Yet, it was the fusion of his passions that found a harmonious outlet in baseball.

His natural athletic prowess not only garnered accolades but also secured him a role as Fritz Ostermueller, one of Jackie Robinson's formidable adversaries, in the acclaimed 2013 feature, "42."

Linc's television journey has left an indelible mark across CBS, HBO, FX, and The CW. Notably, he graced CBS's NCIS as Navy Petty Officer First Class Damien Hunter and is set to enthrall audiences with a recurring role in ABC's Revenge during its final 2013/14 story arc.

From stellar performances alongside Chadwick Boseman and Harrison Ford in "42" to captivating the small screen in fan-favorites like "Revenge" and "NCIS, Hawaii," Linc has been making waves and stealing hearts. However, there's more to him than meets the eye.

Beyond the scripted world, Linc seamlessly transitioned into live comedy on ABC's Jimmy Kimmel Live, sharing the stage with the witty Stephen Merchant during a guest appearance on HBO's Hello Ladies in late 2013.

Balancing the spectrum of his talent, Linc's serious side takes center stage in the 2014 feature "Goodbye World," where he shares the screen with luminaries like Adrian Grenier, Ben McKenzie, and Kid Cudi. This cinematic endeavor opened to acclaim in limited release on April 5, 2014.

In an exclusive interview, we unravel the layers of Linc Hand's fascinating narrative. From his early days as a child actor to his Southern gentleman charm now gracing the bustling city of Los Angeles, Linc bares his soul. Join us as we delve into Exclusive Insights on Balancing Acting and Fitness Success, where Linc shares the highs, lows, and the secrets that shape his resilient journey in conquering Hollywood. So, fasten your seatbelts and embark on this riveting journey into the realm of Linc Hand – where dreams unfold, and every adventure is a spectacle worth savoring.

"I sometimes listen to music while working out, but it's okay if motivation fades, as it happens to everyone. Just focus on your goals, and when things get tough,
keep moving even if it's a little – consistent effort pays off over time, much like water carving through stone. Oh, and there's a song I enjoy playing during my workouts called 'Last Time' by Victoria Renee."

Linc Hand 08 - 34

HI LINC!

YOU'VE HAD AN IMPRESSIVE CAREER IN FILM, SUCH AS "42" WITH CHADWICK BOSEMAN, T.R. KNIGHT, HARRISON FORD, AND TELEVISION, FEATURING IN POPULAR SHOWS LIKE "REVENGE," "TRUE BLOOD," AND "NCIS, HAWAII." WHAT INITIALLY DREW YOU TO ACTING, AND HOW HAS YOUR JOURNEY BEEN IN THE ENTERTAINMENT INDUSTRY?

Linc Hand: Ever since I was a kid, I loved wild adventures. Movies let me live those dreams. My journey's been a crazy ride, full of ups and downs. But you know what? That's what makes the wins so thrilling. It's been one heck of an adventure!

EVER SINCE I WAS A KID, I LOVED WILD ADVENTURES. MOVIES LET ME LIVE THOSE DREAMS. MY JOURNEY'S BEEN A CRAZY RIDE, FULL OF UPS AND DOWNS. BUT YOU KNOW WHAT? THAT'S WHAT MAKES THE WINS SO THRILLING. IT'S BEEN ONE HECK OF AN ADVENTURE!

Linc Hand: Ever since I was a kid, I loved wild adventures. Movies let me live those dreams. My journey's been a crazy ride, full of ups and downs. But you know what? That's what makes the wins so thrilling. It's been one heck of an adventure!

ARE THERE SPECIFIC SKILLS OR TECHNIQUES THEY SHOULD PRIORITIZE DEVELOPING TO EXCEL IN ON-SCREEN PERFORMANCES?

Linc Hand: If you want to be an actor you need to get into acting class and do theater (in my opinion). Just start creating and shooting things even if you use is your phone just go be creative. That's a starting point

BEYOND YOUR ACTING CAREER, YOU'RE KNOWN FOR YOUR DEDICATION TO FITNESS AND EVEN WINNING MUSCLE COMPETITIONS. CAN YOU TELL US MORE ABOUT YOUR FITNESS JOURNEY AND HOW IT COMPLEMENTS YOUR LIFE AS AN ACTOR?

Linc Hand: The gym has always been a major part of my life because of my dad. The gym is my therapy and fitness rolled into one. I enjoy playing physical characters

BALANCING RIGOROUS FITNESS ROUTINES WITH FILMING SCHEDULES CAN BE DEMANDING. HOW DO YOU MANAGE TO MAINTAIN A HEALTHY LIFESTYLE WHILE WORKING IN THE ENTERTAINMENT INDUSTRY?

Linc Hand: It can be difficult sometimes but if you know the WHY you do it then the HOW is not a problem. I try to remember that if I don't want to wake up at 4am to do cardio haha

MANY PEOPLE STRUGGLE WITH STAYING MOTIVATED IN THEIR FITNESS JOURNEY. WHAT ADVICE WOULD YOU GIVE TO INDIVIDUALS AIMING TO ACHIEVE THEIR FITNESS GOALS, ESPECIALLY THOSE JUST STARTING?

Linc Hand: It needs to become a lifestyle not a get in shape quick kind of mindset. Start slow and enjoy the proces

WHAT ROLE HAS FITNESS PLAYED IN YOUR LIFE, NOT JUST PHYSICALLY BUT ALSO MENTALLY AND EMOTIONALLY? HOW DO YOU FIND A BALANCE BETWEEN PHYSICAL HEALTH AND MENTAL WELL-BEING?

Linc Hand: The gym is my safe place. My mental freedom. The weights will never change it is always and will always be the place that gives you back what you give it. It's unconditional

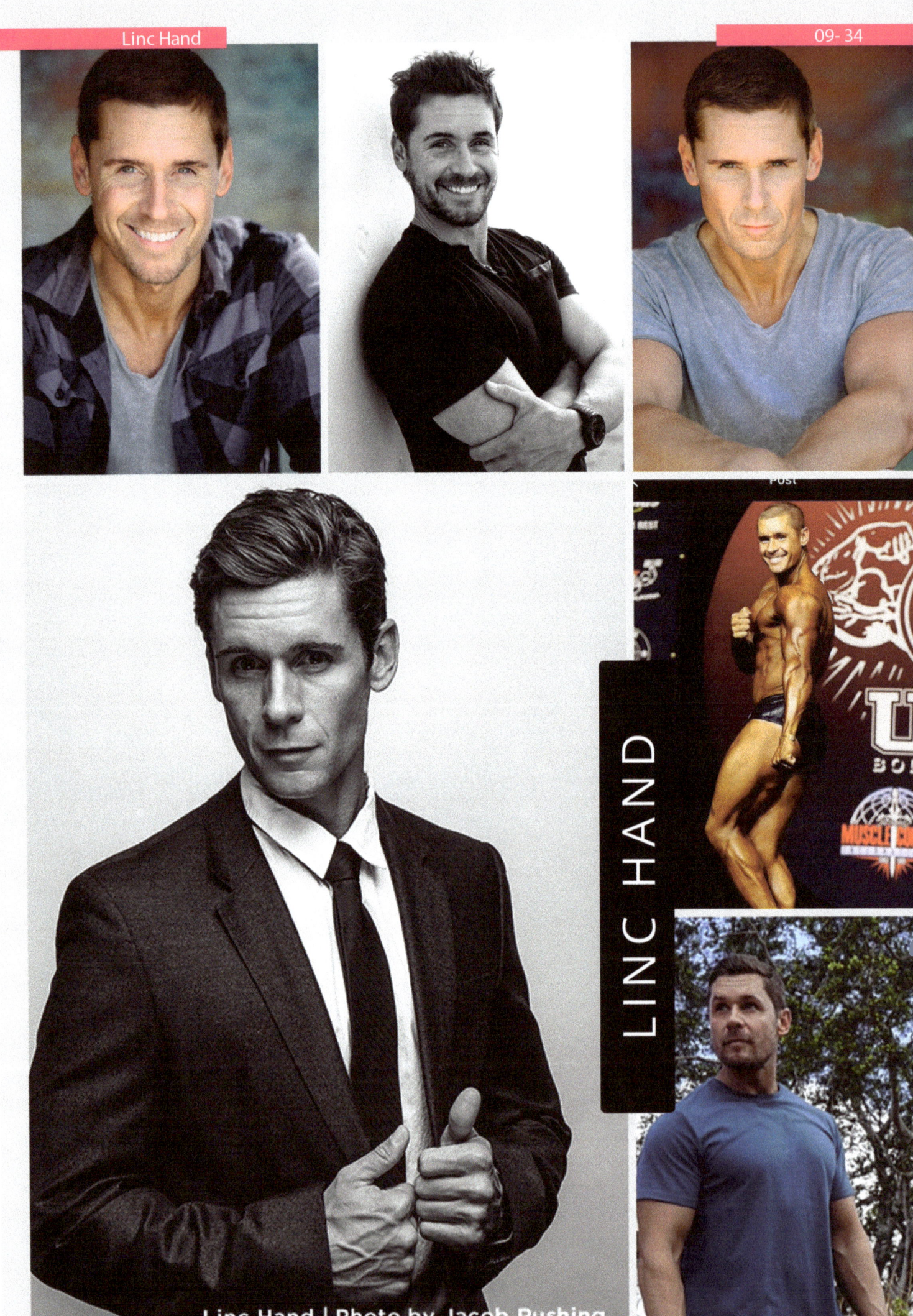

Linc Hand | Photo by Jacob Rushing

L.A. UNLIMITED

APPAREL REPRESENTATION
WITHOUT LIMITS...

- Corporate Brand Representation
- Brand Identity & Management
- Brand Consulting
- Trade Show Preparation & Participation
- Trunk Shows
- Private Label Sales
- Production Sourcing

L.A. Unlimited & Associates
30765 Pacific Coast Hwy STE 443Malibu, CA 90265

310.882.6432
sales@launlimitedinc.com

Editions L.A.

DIGITAL CREATIVE AGENCY

We Transform Your Vision Into Creative Results

Editions L.A. is a full-service agency based in Los Angeles. Our company is a collective of amazing people striving to build delightful services
We believe that is all about getting your message across clearly and with a "Wow!" thrown in for good measure.

Our Awesome Services

Branding

We build, style and tone your brand identity from the ground up.
We rebrand established bands, brands or businesses.

Merchandise Store
Website design and E-Commerce
Website updates

Digital Marketing

CD Cover | Banners | Logo design | Flyers | Brochures | Leaflets | Print ads | Magazine covers & artworks
Facebook / twitter / instagram / youtube artworks
| Book cover
Infographics | Icon Design |
| TshirtsProduct Labels | Presentation slides
Corporate graphics
Professional photo editing & enhancing
Redesign existing elements
YouTube Optimization and Monetization
Youtube Video Editing
Lyric Video and Advertising Design.

Publishing

BOOK COVER DESIGN
EBOOK FORMATTING SERVICES
and distribution on major platforms
(Amazon, Barnes & Nobles..)

Tell us about your dream and we will make it true!

Editions L.A.
7210 Jordan Avenue Suite B42, Canoga Park, California 91303, United States
info@edtions-la.com
Website: www.editions-la.com

Funk Therapy

| Funky | Trendy | Cool | Hip |

Wear The Music You Love!

Visit our merchandise store on our website:
WWW.FUNKTHERAPYMUSIC.COM
10% Discount code: STAYFUNKY

- Hoodies
- Crop Top
- Sweat Pants
- Bucket Hats
- Slides
- Mugs

UNISEX T-SHIRTS

Brown T-Shirt

GRAB IT NOW

Orange T-Shirt

GRAB IT NOW

Beige T-Shirts

GRAB IT NOW

Join our community
@funktherapy2

Beauty

DIY Post-Workout Home Spa: Revive and Recharge

1. CREATE A RELAXING ATMOSPHERE
Dim the lights, light scented candles, and play soft music to set a tranquil ambiance. Consider using essential oil diffusers with calming scents like lavender or eucalyptus to enhance relaxation.

2. SOOTHING BATH TIME
Draw a warm bath and add Epsom salts or a bath bomb to ease tired muscles and relax the body. Consider adding a few drops of essential oils for an aromatic and calming effect.

3. DIY BODY SCRUB
Prepare a homemade exfoliating scrub using sugar or coffee grounds mixed with coconut oil or honey. Gently exfoliate to invigorate your skin and promote circulation.

4. MUSCLE RELIEF SOAK
Fill a basin with warm water and add a few drops of muscle-soothing essential oils like peppermint or rosemary. Soak your feet or hands to ease muscle tension and promote relaxation.

5. NOURISHING FACE MASK
Treat your skin to a hydrating DIY face mask using natural ingredients like yogurt, honey, or mashed avocado. Apply it to revitalize and replenish your skin post-workout.

6. RELAXING TEA BLEND
Sip on a cup of herbal tea known for its calming properties. Chamomile or peppermint tea can help relax your body and mind, complementing your spa experience.

7. GENTLE STRETCHING OR YOGA
Engage in gentle stretching or a brief yoga session to further relax your muscles and improve flexibility. Focus on poses that promote relaxation and restoration

8. MINDFULNESS AND BREATHING EXERCISES
Practice mindfulness or meditation techniques to quiet the mind and deepen relaxation. Incorporate deep breathing exercises to release tension and promote overall calmness.

Wishing you the best with your DIY Post-Workout Home Spa: Revive and Recharge! Remember to prioritize self-care and relish the tranquility that follows. Revel in the sense of being refreshed, revitalized, and prepared to embrace the day ahead with renewed vigor and positivity.

Wellness

NEW YEAR! NEW YOU!

8 BOOKS THAT MAKE YOU FEEL BETTER INSIDE AND OUT

As we embark on a new year, it's the perfect time to set intentions for personal growth and well-being. One powerful way to kickstart this journey is through the transformative magic of books. Here are eight uplifting reads that promise to make you feel better inside and out:

"THE POWER OF NOW" BY ECKHART TOLLE
Genre: Spiritual Growth
Dive into the present moment with Eckhart Tolle's timeless guide. Learn to let go of past regrets and future anxieties, finding peace and fulfillment in the now.

"ATOMIC HABITS" BY JAMES CLEAR
Genre: Self-Help, Productivity
Discover the small changes that lead to remarkable results. James Clear explores the power of habits and how they shape our identity and success.

"THE ALCHEMIST" BY PAULO COELHO
Genre: Autobiography
Join Michelle Obama on her journey from the South Side of Chicago to the White House. Her inspiring story is a testament to resilience, authenticity, and the pursuit of one's dreams.

"The Four Agreements" by Don Miguel Ruiz
Genre: Personal Development, Spirituality
Embrace a code for life based on ancient Toltec wisdom. The Four Agreements offer a powerful guide to personal freedom and a fulfilling existence.

"EAT, PRAY, LOVE" BY ELIZABETH GILBERT
Genre: Memoir
Join Elizabeth Gilbert on her journey of self-discovery across Italy, India, and Indonesia. This memoir is a celebration of life, love, and the pursuit of happiness.

"THE SUBTLE ART OF NOT GIVING A F*CK" BY MARK MANSON
Genre: Self-Help
Mark Manson challenges conventional self-help advice, offering a refreshing perspective on embracing life's challenges and finding meaning in adversity.

"THE BODY KEEPS THE SCORE" BY BESSEL VAN DER KOLK
Genre: Psychology, Trauma
Explore the intricate connection between mind and body. Bessel van der Kolk delves into the effects of trauma and provides insights into healing.

"YOU ARE A BADASS" BY JEN SINCERO
Genre: Self-Help
Unleash your inner badass with Jen Sincero's witty and empowering guide. Discover the keys to personal and financial success while embracing your authentic self.

This new year, nourish your mind and soul with these empowering reads. Each book has the potential to spark positive transformations, leaving you feeling better inside and out. Cheers to a year of growth, resilience, and the joy of discovering the best version of yourself!

FELICIA GREEN

GOD'S PURPOSE

"I realize that my pain was for a bigger purpose and that the plan that God has for me is more important and will help guide others that are in similar situations."

WWW.FELICIAGREEN.COM
@AUTHORFELICIAGREEN

VACATIONS
WHERE YOU CAN RELAX AND STAY HEALTHY

In our fast-paced lives, vacations offer a precious opportunity to unwind, rejuvenate, and prioritize our well-being. Instead of simply seeking escape, more travelers are now opting for destinations that not only provide relaxation but also support a healthy lifestyle. Here's a curated list of vacation spots that promise serenity, relaxation, and a focus on staying healthy:

1. TROPICAL YOGA RETREATS
Retreats nestled in serene tropical locations offer more than just picturesque landscapes. They provide yoga sessions, meditation, and wellness programs that encourage mental and physical rejuvenation. Destinations like Bali, Costa Rica, or Thailand are popular choices for such retreats.

2. SPA GETAWAYS
Indulge in a luxurious spa getaway where pampering meets wellness. These destinations offer an array of spa treatments, from massages to hydrotherapy, aimed at relieving stress, promoting relaxation, and revitalizing the body. Consider locations such as Sedona, Arizona, or the Blue Lagoon in Iceland.

3. MOUNTAIN WELLNESS RETREATS
For those seeking a tranquil escape amidst nature, mountain wellness retreats offer fresh air, stunning vistas, and a range of activities like hiking, meditation, and forest bathing. Destinations like the Swiss Alps, the Rocky Mountains, or the Himalayas provide an ideal setting for such retreats.

4. HEALTHY CULINARY TOURS
Explore destinations known for their healthy and flavorful cuisines. Opt for culinary tours that not only offer delicious meals but also educate on nutritious eating habits. Places like Japan, Greece, or Italy offer unique culinary experiences emphasizing fresh, local ingredients.

5. MINDFUL MEDITATION ESCAPES
Discover destinations that specialize in mindfulness and meditation practices. Retreats focused on mindfulness offer a serene environment conducive to self-reflection and inner peace. Locations such as Sedona, Arizona, or the temples of Kyoto, Japan, are ideal for such serene escapes.

6. WELLNESS RESORTS WITH FITNESS PROGRAMS
Wellness resorts that combine relaxation with fitness programs offer a balanced approach to vacationing. From yoga and Pilates to personalized fitness sessions, these resorts cater to those seeking a blend of relaxation and physical activity. Consider destinations like California's Napa Valley or the Swiss
countryside.

7. BEACHSIDE HEALTH RETREATS
Opt for health retreats located by the sea, offering a perfect harmony of relaxation and well-being. Activities like beach yoga, surfing, or simply soaking up the sun contribute to a rejuvenating experience. Destinations like Hawaii, the Maldives, or the Caribbean are popular choices for beachside wellness.

8. NATURE IMMERSION AND ECO-RETREATS
Immerse yourself in nature and sustainable living at eco-retreats. Experience outdoor activities, eco-friendly practices, and a deep connection with nature in locations like Costa Rica's rainforests or Norway's fjords.

May your next vacation be a journey not just for the body, but also for the soul. You deserve the gift of relaxation and well-being. Choose to return home refreshed and inspired, ready to embrace life's adventures with a renewed sense of vitality and joy.

EXPLORE
The World

WHY YOU SHOULD CONSIDER TRAVELING IN A MOTOR HOME

Freedom

When you travel with a motor home, you have the ultimate freedom to explore the world. You can go wherever you want, when you want and stay as long as you desire. No need to worry about finding a place to stay, looking for public transportation or dealing with airline tickets!

Affordability

You'll save money on accommodation since you'll be staying in your own self-contained living space. You'll also save money on food costs since you'll have a fully functioning kitchen in your motor home. Not to mention, you'll save money on transport as your motor home will get you from point A to point B.

Comfort

You will have access to a full kitchen, living area, sleeping quarters and bathroom, all in one vehicle. This means that you won't have to worry about packing up your things each time you move from one place to another. Plus, you don't have to worry about expensive hotel bills when you stay on the road for long periods of time.

BOOK NOW

- 123981 Craftsman Rd., Calabasas, CA 91302
- 1(818) 225-8239
- www.expeditionmotorhomes.com/

Mantras to make You Feel Strong & Unstoppable

In the journey of life, many of us face moments where we doubt our worth and feel belittled by our inner critic or external opinions. Low self-esteem can cloud our perception of ourselves, affecting our confidence and overall well-being. However, amidst these challenges, affirmations serve as powerful tools to uplift our spirits and cultivate a more positive self-image. Here are ten simple yet impactful affirmations tailored to bolster self-esteem:

1. "I AM IMPORTANT, AND I MATTER."
This affirmation reminds us that our presence and contributions hold significance, regardless of external judgments.

2. "I AM GOOD ENOUGH JUST AS I AM."
Embracing self-acceptance, this affirmation reinforces the belief that we are inherently worthy and deserving.

3. "I CAN DO GREAT THINGS."
Believing in our capabilities fuels motivation and encourages us to embrace opportunities with confidence.

4. "I BELIEVE IN MYSELF."
Self-belief serves as a foundation for self-esteem, fostering trust in our abilities and decisions.

5. "I DESERVE RESPECT."
Acknowledging our worthiness of respect reinforces boundaries and self-value in interactions with others.

6. "I AM VALUABLE."
Recognizing our inherent value encourages a mindset shift towards self-appreciation and self-care.

7. "I AM STRONG AND CAPABLE."
This affirmation reinforces our resilience and ability to navigate challenges with strength and competence.

8. "I AM WORTHY OF LOVE AND KINDNESS."
Affirming our deserving nature of love and kindness encourages nurturing positive relationships and self-compassion.

9. "I AM PROUD OF WHO I AM."
Celebrating our strengths and achievements fosters a sense of pride and self-acknowledgment.

10. "I AM BECOMING BETTER EVERY DAY."
Encouraging personal growth, this affirmation embraces the journey of self-improvement and learning.

Repeating these affirmations regularly, especially during moments of self-doubt, helps rewire negative thought patterns and cultivates a more positive self-image. Remember, these affirmations are not about denying challenges but empowering oneself to face them with greater confidence and self-assuredness.

By integrating these affirmations into daily routines, we can gradually transform our inner dialogue and cultivate a stronger, more resilient sense of self. Embrace these affirmations, let them resonate within you, and witness the positive impact they can have on your self-esteem and overall well-being.

www.kpiuradio.com

Pump it up
magazine radio

Tune in everyday 3.00pm - 6.00 pm(pst)
11.00pm - 4.00am(pst)

Indie Artist Top 8 Chart — fitness warriors playlist

1. Gonna Be Alright
   Aneessa

2. Victoria Renee
   Last Time

3. Old School Party
   Funk Therapy feat. Michael B. Sutton

4. Rising
   Mitchell Coleman Jr.

5. Randy White
   Focus

6. Fernando Harkless
   Sticks & Stones

7. Superwoman
   Anya Rose

8. De Volta a 1984
   Dj GMS

Available Also on AMAZON ALEXA Simply ask: "Alexa, Play Pump it up Magazine Radio from Tunein"

KPIU RADIO
THE WEST COAST WAVE

Pump It Up Magazine Radio is proud to honor independent artists

www.kpiuradio.com

FITNESS 22- 34

BRING YOUR BODY IN SHAPE

JUST DO IT!

Body Shape Workout

Pump it up Magazine / 22 - 34

10 MINUTES ABS WORKOUT

SIT UP
3 SET 10 REPS

LEG RAISES
3 SET 10 REPS

CRUNCH HOLD
3 SET 10 REPS

PLANK
3 SET 10 REPS

@pumpitupmagazine

NEW YEAR, NEW YOU!
HOW TO BREAK FREE FROM NARCISSISTIC ABUSE

Abuse comes in many forms, whether it's from a parent, spouse, friend, or anyone else. No matter the relationship, abuse is still abuse. As the new year begins, it's essential to recognize that healing from narcissistic abuse is possible, and there are steps you can take to start anew.

1. RECOGNIZE THE ABUSE
Identify signs of manipulation and control in your relationship. Understanding this behavior is the first step towards change.

2. SEEK SUPPORT
Talk to someone you trust—a friend, family member, or therapist. Support from others can make a big difference in your healing journey.

3. SET BOUNDARIES
Create clear rules about what behavior is acceptable. Setting limits can protect you from further harm.

4. SELF-CARE AND HEALING METHODS

a. Therapeutic Frequencies and Binaural Beats
Listening to calming music with therapeutic frequencies or binaural beats can help reduce stress and anxiety. They're like soothing sounds for your mind.

b. Hypnotherapy Sessions
Consider hypnotherapy, a therapy that uses deep relaxation techniques to help cope with trauma. It might bring hidden answers to light.

c. Emotion Code Sessions
This method helps release trapped emotions from past experiences. It's like decluttering emotional baggage to feel lighter and more at peace.

5. LEARN ABOUT NARCISSISTIC ABUSE
Understanding more about narcissistic abuse can empower you to make better choices for yourself and regain control of your life.

6. REBUILDING CONFIDENCE
Abuse can make you doubt yourself. Rediscover what makes you unique and special. Celebrate your strengths and talents.

7. SURROUND YOURSELF WITH POSITIVE PEOPLE
Spend time with those who genuinely care about you. Positive relationships can provide much-needed support and encouragement.

8. TAKE SMALL STEPS TOWARD HEALING
Healing takes time. Be patient with yourself and take small, manageable steps towards a healthier and happier life.

Remember that abuse, regardless of its form or the relationship it stems from, is never acceptable. It's crucial to recognize the impact it has had on your life and take steps towards healing and liberation. You deserve to live a life free from the shackles of manipulation and mistreatment. May this new year be a chapter of resilience, self-love, and renewed hope—a chapter where you write your story of triumph over adversity. Let it be the year where you embrace a new you—a you who is strong, empowered, and deserving of every happiness life has to offer.

Tips For Taking Care Of Your
MENTAL HEALTH
C-PTSD & NARCISSISTIC ABUSE

People who have Narcissistic Personality Disorder have damaged self-esteem that is easily harmed by even small criticisms.
They are continually looking to shore up their weak areas of self-opinion.
To accomplish this need for self-preservation, they abuse and use other people, including, unfortunately, their own children, significant others etc..

Recognize the trait of the narcissist
- A sense of uniqueness
- Boastful behavior
- Exaggeration of their talents
- Grandiose fantasies
- A sense of superiority
- Self-centered behavior
- Self-referential behavior
- A deep need for attention and admiration

Recognize the trait of The covert narcissist
- Passive Self-Importance
- Blaming and Shaming
- Creating Confusion
- Procrastination and Disregard (The covert narcissist is a professional at not acknowledging you at all.)
- Giving With a Goal (to make themselves look good)
- Emotionally Neglectful

How to Deal With a Narcissist
- Set Boundaries
- Avoid Taking It Personally
- Advocate for Yourself
- Create a Healthy Distance
- Seek Help – Talk to a Therapist
- Remove the Heart Wall
- Emotion Codean energy healing technique for releasing trapped emotion

C-PTSD
Complex Post Traumatic Stress Disorder
is more severe if:
- the traumatic events happened early in life
- the trauma was caused by a wife/husband/parent
- the person experienced the trauma for a long time
- the person was alone during the trauma
- there's still contact with the person responsible for the trauma

Symptoms of complex PTSD
- Anxiety - Agoraphobia - Panic Attack
- Alcoholism - Drug Abuse
- Negative thoughts about yourself, other people or the world
- Hopelessness about the future
- Memory problems,
- Difficulty maintaining close relationships
- Feeling detached from family and friends
- Lack of interest in activities you once enjoyed
- Difficulty experiencing positive emotions
- Feeling emotionally numb

How to Treat complex PTSD
- Set Boundaries
- Avoid Taking It Personally
- Advocate for Yourself
- Create a Healthy Distance
- Seek Help – Talk to a Therapist
- Remove the Heart Wall with the help of a Healer

@pumpitupmagazine
www.pumpitupmagazine.com

> THE WEEKEND by NATHAN X

Energetic, upbeat and brimming with positive vibes;
A pop-perfect anthem lands somewhere between piano house and tech house. All topped off with the beautifully soaring and soulful vocals of up and coming singer CHAR. It's impossible to listen to this dance-floor banger without at the very least nodding your head. The perfect companion to anyone looking to get hyped for a good time. With the alluringly infectious hook "Everybody loves the weekend" likely to get stuck in your head for weeks to come.

Pump it up Magazine

NATHAN X
"THE WEEKEND"
OUT NOW!

8 TRANSFORMATIVE FILMS FOR HEALING AND RETHINKING REALITY

In a world often inundated with the chaos of everyday life, seeking solace and perspective become essential. Cinema, as an art form, has the remarkable ability to transport us beyond our own experiences, prompting introspection and inspiring personal growth. Here are eight extraordinary films that not only entertain but also serve as catalysts for healing and a profound reconsideration of reality.

"Eternal Sunshine of the Spotless Mind" (2004) - Director: Michel Gondry
Synopsis: This unconventional love story explores the intricacies of memory and heartache. Through its surreal narrative, it delves into the depths of human emotions and the complexities of relationships, offering insights into the healing power of acceptance and letting go.

"The Truman Show" (1998) - Director: Peter Weir
Synopsis: In a thought-provoking portrayal of a man unaware that his life is a televised reality show, this film challenges our perceptions of authenticity and free will. It encourages viewers to question the nature of their own realities and the influences that shape them.

"The Matrix" (1999) - Directors: The Wachowskis
Synopsis: A groundbreaking sci-fi film that questions the essence of reality itself. Through its gripping narrative and mind-bending visuals, it invites audiences to contemplate the nature of existence and the concept of a simulated reality.

"Waking Life" (2001) - Director: Richard Linklater
Synopsis: An animated journey through various philosophical conversations, this film presents an exploration of dreams, consciousness, and the nature of reality. Its dreamlike visuals and thought-provoking dialogues offer a unique perspective on existence.

"Into the Wild" (2007) - Director: Sean Penn
Synopsis: Based on a true story, this film follows a young man's journey of self-discovery as he abandons societal conventions to explore the wilderness. It prompts reflection on the pursuit of meaning, freedom, and the essence of human connection.

"Her" (2013) - Director: Spike Jonze
Synopsis: Set in a near-future world, this unconventional love story between a man and an operating system delves into themes of loneliness, human connection, and the evolving relationship between technology and emotions.

"Inception" (2010) - Director: Christopher Nolan
Synopsis: Through its complex narrative about entering dreams within dreams, this film challenges perceptions of reality, blurring the lines between the conscious and subconscious. It's an intriguing exploration of the power of the mind and the nature of perception.

"Samsara" (2011) - Director: Ron Fricke
Synopsis: This visually stunning documentary, devoid of dialogue and narrative, takes viewers on a transcendent journey across diverse cultures and landscapes. It prompts contemplation on the interconnectedness of humanity and the beauty of the world we inhabit.

These cinematic gems serve as more than mere entertainment; they are powerful tools for introspection and healing. Through their thought-provoking narratives and captivating visuals, they encourage audiences to reconsider their perceptions of reality, fostering personal growth and emotional well-being. So, grab some popcorn, settle in, and let these movies take you on a transformative journey—one that might just change how you perceive the world around you.

HONORING DR. MARTIN LUTHER KING JR.:
SUPPORTING BLACK COMMUNITIES AND HOW YOU CAN HELP

As we commemorate the legacy of Dr. Martin Luther King Jr., it is essential to reflect not only on the strides made in the fight against racial injustice but also on the ongoing challenges faced by Black communities. In this article, we will explore meaningful ways to honor Dr. King's vision, support Black communities, and discuss actionable steps that everyone can take to contribute to positive change

DR. KING'S LEGACY AND ITS CONTEMPORARY RELEVANCE

Highlight Dr. King's monumental contributions to the Civil Rights Movement and underscore the timeless relevance of his principles. Explore how embracing equality, justice, and unity can significantly impact supporting Black communities today.

IDENTIFYING ONGOING CHALLENGES IN BLACK COMMUNITIES

Delve into the systemic issues persisting in Black communities, including economic disparities, educational inequalities, and social injustices. Understanding these challenges is crucial for developing effective strategies to address and overcome them.

Top Tips for Supporting Black Communities

A) TIP 1: EDUCATE YOURSELF ACTIVELY:
Encourage individuals to proactively educate themselves on the history of racial inequality and systemic racism. Provide top resources for reading, watching documentaries, and engaging in meaningful conversations to foster awareness.

B) TIP 2: SUPPORT BLACK-OWNED BUSINESSES:
Emphasize the significance of patronizing Black entrepreneurs and businesses to boost economic empowerment within the community. Offer top tips for finding and supporting Black-owned establishments.

C) TIP 3: ENGAGE LOCALLY:
Advocate for community involvement by sharing top tips for participating in local initiatives addressing racial disparities. Highlight volunteer opportunities, neighborhood programs, and grassroots organizations as effective ways to make a difference.

D) TIP 4: FOSTER DIVERSITY AND INCLUSION:
Provide actionable tips for promoting diversity and inclusion in various settings, from workplaces to educational institutions. Offer insights on creating environments that celebrate differences and advocate for equality.

E) TIP 5: CONTRIBUTE FINANCIALLY TO CHARITIES:
Share top tips for making a meaningful impact by donating to reputable organizations supporting Black communities. Highlight the collective power of financial contributions and provide information on trusted charities.

Conclusion:
Honoring Dr. Martin Luther King Jr. requires more than passive acknowledgment; it necessitates active participation in the ongoing fight against racial injustice. By following these top tips, we can collectively contribute to Dr. King's dream of a more just and equal society. Let us be agents of positive change, applying these actionable steps to empower Black communities and work towards a future guided by justice and equality.

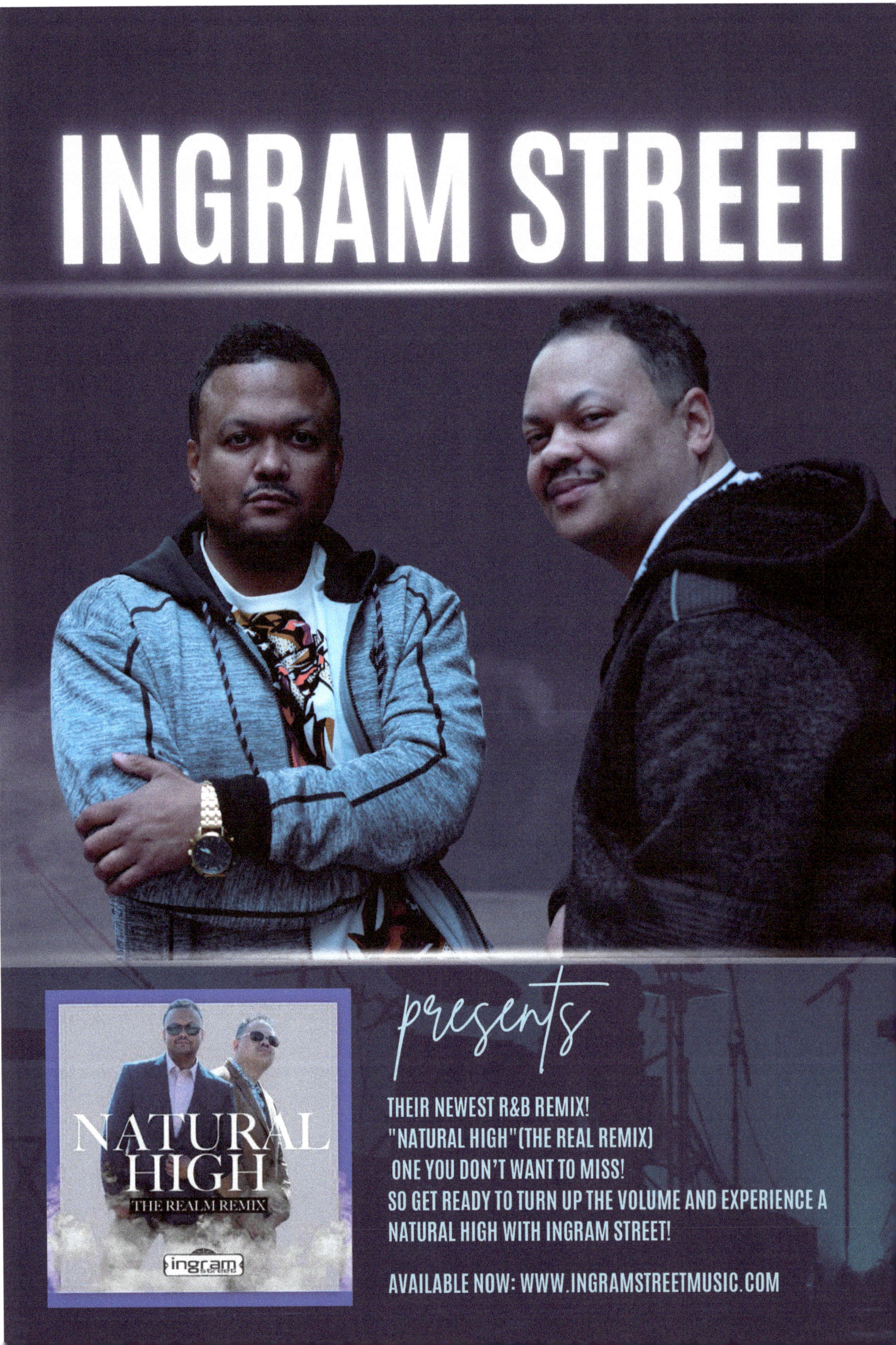

AN AMERICAN GAL'S COOKBOOK: DISCOVERING DELICIOUS RECIPES AND FASCINATING HISTORIES ACROSS THE 50 STATES BY BOBBI JO LATHAN

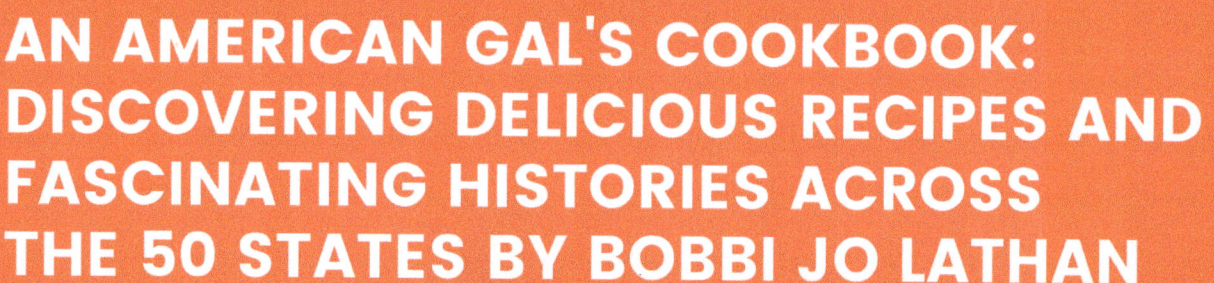

COOK NOW

WEST END ORGANIX

Ageless Beauty, Organic Health

Look and feel younger and healthier with our natural remedies products!

www.WestEndOrganix.com

Discount: 10% off of your order - Code *WEO2021*

www.ingramcontent.com/pod-product-compliance
Lightning Source LLC
LaVergne TN
LVHW072252060526
838201LV00070B/4975